Don't Go To Hell From The Church

By:

Penelope "Minister P." Taylor

Don't Go To Hell From The Church

By

Penelope "Minister P." Taylor

Copyright @ 2019, All Rights Reserved
Printed in The United States of America

Published By:

ABM Publications
A division of Andrew Bills Ministries Inc.
PO Box 6811, Orange, CA 92863

ISBN: 978-1-931820-92-9

All scripture quotations, unless otherwise indicated are taken from the King James Version of the Bible, Public Domain. Those marked AMP are from the Amplified Bible, copyright @ 1987, The Updated Edition, by the Zondervan Corporation and the Lockman Foundation, and is used by permission. All rights reserved.

Acknowledgements

As I always say to God be the Glory for all the things He has done and is doing in my life. Thanks to my husband, my children and my grandchildren for always supporting me. Thanks to my church family Walking by Faith Ministry. Thanks to my family and friends for investing so much in me. Thanks to God's COVER GIRLS you guys ROCK!!! Women of Destiny you already know I love you. Thanks to my Facebook Ministry that God has assigned me with in this season.

I love you all

Minister P.

PENELOPE "MINISTER P." TAYLOR

TABLE OF CONTENTS

1	Sound The Alarm	7
2	Stop Living In The Past	13
3	Don't Go To Hell From The Church	17
4	Church Folks Gone Wild	21
5	God Will Give You Direction	29
6	Keep It Moving	33
7	Punks And Pimps In The Pulpit	37
8	Thugs In The Church	41
9	Loose Women In The Church	43
10	Nuggets From The Prophet	47
11	No More Excuses	49
12	Put A Praise On It	53
	About The Author	61
	Contact Information	62

CHAPTER 1

SOUND THE ALARM

As you begin to read this book, please read from front to back.

I thank God that He inspired me to write a third book representing the Trinity; God the Father, God the Son and God the Holy Spirit. That's who He is to me. God's desire is that none of us would be lost, but we all will come to know Him.

Readers Meditate on this.

Mark Chapter 1 verse 15 says the time is fulfilled, and the Kingdom of God is at hand. REPENT and believe in the gospel. REPENT WHAT? Repent of your sin.

What is this scripture saying? It's telling us two things we need to do. REPENT and BELIEVE. If we don't REPENT and BELIEVE Guess What? We will be lost. We can't repent without believing and we can't believe without repenting. Why? Because they both go together, that's what the scripture says. You must believe in the gospel, and the gospel is Jesus Christ which is THE GOOD NEWS! It says that the time is fulfilled, meaning the time has come to SOUND THE ALARM.
Not tomorrow, not yesterday, but today right now.

Let me give you a few scriptures for your study time. Jot

them down so you can go back for your reference.

Matthew 3:2 says REPENT, here it is again. For the kingdom of heaven has come near.

Acts 2:38 Peter also Replies. REPENT and be baptized every one of you in the name of Jesus Christ for the forgiveness of your sins and you will receive the gift of the Holy Spirit.

This has now been witnessed to at the proper time.

Now what are these scriptures saying? It's letting us know that the alarm has gone off. Jesus is sounding the alarm. He wants everybody 1st Timothy 2:6 says Jesus, who gave himself as a ransom for all people. to know that the kingdom is at hand. Now is the time to get right with God. Not tomorrow because tomorrow is not promise to any of us. Do it right now. God is a right now God waiting to receive you as His own. IT'S TIME TO SOUND THE ALARM.

Their message can be simply put in one word, REPENT!

Throughout the Bible we are told to repent for the sins we have committed and turn to the Lord. The Bible tells us that we are to believe, confess, repent and be baptized and then do what? Live a life Holy and Pleasing unto God. People don't want to live Holy anymore. Preachers don't preach hell and damnation anymore. But let me tell you one thing readers. PLEASE DON'T GO TO HELL FROM THE CHURCH.

This is a message that we need to Preach to the people, not only of salvation, but also of repentance.

Matthew chapter 3 verse 1-2 says "In those days John the Baptist came, preaching in the Desert of Judea and saying, "Repent for the kingdom of heaven is near."

Let me tell you who John the Baptist was…. John the Baptist was the forerunner who prepared the way for the Lord. He was letting the people know that the Messiah would come, not that a Savior would come to bring peace and justice to this earth, conquering its opposition, but also to REPENT.

John the Baptist was simply letting the people know what they should have already known, because that is exactly what the Old Testament said would happen, but they didn't realize the message. For us we know that the Savior came and went to the cross and died, but on the third day rose from the grave, walked out of the tomb and is in heaven with the Father and will one day come back to take His children home, not just because the Bible says so, but for the way those who proclaimed this message lived. We know that one day we are going to go before God who sits on the Judgment seat, but we do not live or act as though that is going to take place anytime soon.

You see along with Jesus came the dawning of the kingdom. He is so close to coming back to take us home that even Jesus said what John the Baptist said. Do you all remember what happened on 911? The event of 911 should be a warning to us. The event of that tragic day should tell us we are in the end times. Jesus said we were in the end times since the days of John the Baptist. Today we must do what John did; today we who are in Christ are the watchmen, today we are to prepare the people for the SECOND COMING. We are to prepare people and let them know that Jesus is coming back and they need to repent and turn their lives around, but before we can ask them to do that, before we can go and ask them to repent and turn their lives around we must make sure our lives are right with God first. It's time for the people of God to begin to Practice WHAT WE PREACH. We must make sure that we are living a life Holy and Pleasing unto God before we can ask others to do that. We need to make sure that we are doing His will and not our own will, but too often that is not the case; too often we do what we want to do and not what the Lord wants us to do.

Need I remind you what the Lord said about being lukewarm Christians? We must not play church or the role of a Christian. We cannot just go to church on Sundays, Tuesdays and Wednesdays and expect to get into heaven or say that we are Christians. We must be about our Father's business and stop sitting on the stool of do nothing waiting for someone else to do something that God has called us to do. It's time to stop shucking and jiving with our salvation. People are going to hell in a hand basket and the people of God are still sitting in our stained-glass beautiful sanctuary having church as usual. It's time for us to go into the hedged and the highways and compel the people to come.

Let me tell you something right now. You can have all the money in the world, drive the nicest car, live in the finest homes, have every color Michael Kors bag there is, or have all the fame in the world, but if you do not have Christ then you have nothing, except a free pass to hell. It doesn't matter whether we are the most popular person in town or in church on Sunday morning, if we don't have Christ in our life, if we do not have a personal relationship with Him and do not do His will then we are going to HELL.

It's time for us to SOUND THE ALARM and let the people know that judgment is coming! Preachers don't want to preach judgment anymore, they WANT TO PREACH HOW MUCH MONEY YOU GOING TO RECEIVE IN THE MAIL NEXT WEEK, OR YOU GOING TO BE BLESSED WITH A SIX FIGURE JOB. ALL THAT'S GOOD, but if you don't have Jesus, GUESS WHAT? You still are going to HELL.

Mark 8:36 says what would it profit a man to gain the whole world and turn around and lose His soul?

If that happens shame on you, it will be nobody fault but your own. Once you take your last breath it will be to late. Make your election sure. The choice is yours. Choose this day who you are going to serve. We never know when the Lord will call our name. I have lost family members this year, I have lost some very dear friends this year, but I thank God they died in Christ. Some were old and some were young. There is no age limit when it comes to death and hell. Never think you are too old or to young to be used by God.

Let me tell you a few people God used to sound the alarm in the bible.

God used John The Baptist to sound the alarm telling the people to repent.

God used the prophet Hosea to sound the alarm to His people (Hosea 5:8) that punishment was coming.

God used Joel to sound the alarm that the lord was coming.

God used Peter to sound the alarm.

God used James to sound the alarm.

God used Isaiah to sound the alarm.

God used Ezekiel to sound the alarm.

God used Moses to sound the alarm.

God used Amos to sound the alarm.

 Now if God can use all these great men in the bible to sound the alarm what makes you think He can't use you? When God tells us to sound the alarm, He's telling us to let the people know that the kingdom of God is at hand.

God is true to His word and the devil is a lie. The devil wants to counterfeit Gods word by making you believe the lies that he whispers in your ear. Let me warn my readers again, if you end up in hell it will be nobody fault but your own, come to Jesus while you still have time. It's time to wake up. THE ALARM HAS BEEN SOUND.

CHAPTER 2

STOP LIVING IN THE PAST

Your past has no business telling your future what the outcome will be. We all have a right to dream, and we all have a right to go after our dream, but to often people and conditions will try to interrupt or slow our excitement down. Just because you do not have a vision and a plan for your future stop trying to hold others back from reaching their dream. Most people don't have a problem as long as you are sitting down doing nothing, but the minute you make up your mind that you want a better future is when the enemy gets mad at you and people get jealous at what God wants to do in your life.

The enemy is very crafty in his approach. What did he tell Eve? He told Eve if she ate the forbidden fruit, she would not surely die. Keep believing that lie if you want to and see want you end up in hell. He was putting disbelief in her mind. The enemy knew Adam and Eve had a vision and a purpose to fulfill, just like he knows you and I have a vision and a purpose to fulfill, but his mission was to kill the plan of God.

The enemy wants to kill your purpose by keeping your mind stuck in the past. Remember what you did ten years ago. Remember when you were on drugs, remember when you were out there prostituting, remember when you were out there running behind them men, and remember when you were out there chasing women. It's time to stop living in the past and be all you can be for the Glory of God. Don't worry about your yesterday, for yesterday is gone, so learn how to keep it moving and stay focus on God and His plan for your life.

Matthew 6:34 says take therefore no thought for the morrow: for the morrow shall take thought for the things of itself. Sufficient unto the day is the evil thereof.

We don't have to worry about anything because God has already made everything possible for us who believe. Each day has enough problems of its own. If God cares for the lilies of the field don't you know He cares for you? God told us not to worry so why can't we believe what He says? Worrying will suck the life out of you and keep you drained. If you cast your cares on the Lord, He will take care of you. Stop worrying about friends that does not have your best interest to heart. Some of your closest friends and associates are just like that serpent in the Garden of Eden, trying to get you to doubt just enough to set you back from walking in your purpose.

God wants you to live and have the best life ever, but in order to do that you can't continue to hang around the same old negative people that keep feeding negativity into your spirit. There comes a time in life where you must move from around some people. I know tough decisions are hard to make sometimes. You think that's your home girl or your road dog, but when God says its time to move, when you hear the voice of God harden not your heart, listen to His voice and move. In the end it will be worth the effort. Don't let your past paralyze you from walking into your divine purpose.

You need to begin to see yourself as God sees you. You need to see yourself happy, successful, and prosperous. Don't allow anyone to talk you out of what God has for you.

I learned a long time ago that what God has for me is for me and can't a devil in hell take what God has for me. We've got to get past what people think about us. What does God think about me is what you should be asking yourself? If you are doing the will of Jesus Christ people shouldn't be your problem.

God want us to stand when everything around us may be falling apart. When you know you have done all you can do STAND ANYWAY. Oppositions will come. But know that you have a Savior, His name is Jesus Christ and He will see you through. Now is your time to shine for the Lord. Again, I say! STOP LIVING IN THE PAST.

PENELOPE "MINISTER P." TAYLOR

CHAPTER 3

Don't Go to Hell FROM THE CHURCH

There are so many people sitting in the house of God and on their way to hell. Listen people just because you are a Preacher does not guarantee you a seat in heaven. Just because you are a Missionary or an Evangelist does not mean you are going to heaven. If the truth be told a lot of people sitting in the pulpit are on their way to hell. We preach the word to others Sunday after Sunday, but our lifestyle is not lining up with the word of God.

There will come a time when Preachers will have to preach what the government tells them to Preach if they are receiving grants from them. I would hate to die and go to hell because of what the government told me I had to Preach. I do not want the Lord to tell me to depart because He never knew me. That will be a dreadful day to anyone that will have to experience that.

It's time for us to believe that Jesus is who He says He is.

People let me warn you. DON'T GO TO HELL FROM THE CHURCH.

Mark 8:29 says: who do people say that I am? Peter replies; "You are the Christ."

There is great power and authority in knowing who you are. It's that power and authority that says, regardless of what my past looks like I will continue to trust God for my future. If you keep your mind on God success will happen for you. I never thought I would be an Author, but I thank God for the Blessings of Abraham being upon my life. Whatever God says we can have, believe me, we can have it. It's time to stop feeling sorry for yourself and seek God so that He can give you direction for your life. Do you really believe what the word of God says? If you do you will know that you are an overcomer through Christ Jesus. You will know that No Weapon formed against you will prosper. You will know that because Jesus lives you can face tomorrow. Sometimes you got to remind God what His word says about you. The devil does not want you to believe the report of the Lord.

James 4:7 says Submit yourselves therefore to God. Resist the devil, and he will flee from you.

You don't have to let the devil pick on you. God has given you a way of escape through His written word.

You have been given power over the adversary. When the enemy says you have no future, tell him to go to H**L!

IT'S TIME FOR THE PEOPLE OF GOD TO DRAW CLOSER TO GOD NOW MORE THAN EVER, AND FOR THOSE THAT DO NOT KNOW THE LORD IT'S TIME YOU GET TO KNOW HIM BECAUSE PERILOUS TIMES ARE ALREADY HERE.

James 4:8 says "Draw near to God and He will draw near to you"

One way you can draw near to God is to get rid of pride and cleanse your hands from sin.

We cannot resist the devil without God's help because our flesh won't let us.

When you want to tip over to Brother John Doe's house or Sister Mary's house your flesh will tell you its ok, but your spirit will tell you that man or that woman doesn't belongs to you. When you want to go the club or the bar and hang out with the fellows or your best girlfriend your flesh will tell you its okay, but your spirit will tell you that you have been changed and that you are a new creature in Christ Jesus. You see your Spirit man wants to do the right thing but sometimes your flesh won't let it. My father used to tell me all the time which ever one that you feed the most will always be the strongest. If you don't stay in the word you will continue to get weak and when you get weak is when the devil will try all he can to move in and take up residence in your life. God has given us a way of escape but it's up to you to take it.

PEOPLE PLEASE DON'T GO TO HELL FROM THE CHURCH.

You want people to follow you as a leader, but when they see the life and the example that you are setting makes them want no part of being a Christian. We as believers should to be able to draw others to Christ. We should be letting our light shine before men so that they may see our good works and the father in heaven will be glorified. Look at the scripture for yourself.

Matthew 5:16 says, Let your light so shine before men, that they may see your good works, and glorify your Father which is in heaven.

This is what the word of God says.

Why would you want to put your light under a bushel when it can shine? God is so sick and tired of church folks playing church. I think my next book I write will be about church folks gone wild, better yet I think I will add a chapter in this book CHURCH FOLKS GONE WILD Keep reading, the best is yet to come.

CHAPTER 4

CHURCH FOLKS GONE WILD

Before you readers finish this book, I pray that GOD WILL CONVICT YOUR SPIRIT THAT YOU DON'T HAVE TO GO TO HELL FROM THE CHURCH. God has been warning us over and over again. He's been giving us time and time again to get it right. Everyday that we open our eyes is a new day for us to get it right with God.

Jeremiah 7:23 King James Version (KJV) reads:

[23] But this thing commanded I them, saying, Obey my voice, and I will be your God, and ye shall be my people: and walk ye in all the ways that I have commanded you, that it may be well unto you.

The first thing we must do is to obey the voice of the Lord. I don't know about you, but I want things to be well unto me.

What is wrong with the body of Christ is that we are listening at too many voices that we can't hear the voice of the Lord. We need to pray and ask God what it is He wants us to do and what He does not want us to do. If we follow Gods lead our day and our life will be so much better and it will run so much smoother.

If you don't do what God wants you to do, you will begin

to listen to people and let them manipulate you into doing what they want you to do. If that happens you will end up doing things you were never anointed to do. If you do what God wants you to do you will be blessed with everything you need to get the job done. He will bless you with love, joy, peace, longsuffering, rest and great relationships with people that He allows to cross your path.

We've got to many distractions going on within the body of Christ. The world puts enough distractions in our way, but then when you look at the church you say... CHURCH FOLKS GONE WILD! BEWARE OF CHURCH FOLKS!

We talk about church folks and saved folks so let's not get it twisted. There is a difference between church folks and saved folks. Church folks have not been spiritually fed on the word of God that's why they've gone wild. They are anorexia Christians, they take garbage from church to church, no matter what program you put them on they can't work with nobody. They never have a good day and everyday of there life they have something to complain about. Beware of people who can't stand to see things going good.

There are too many church folks falling by the wayside. There are too many church folks falling for the lies of this world. We are living in the last days and we must be prepared spiritually for the end times. God has told us in His word everything that will happen in the last days and yet we always fail to have a death ear. Why can't we just believe Him? We sit in our churches Sunday after Sunday listening to what the Preacher is saying, but are we taking notes and applying the word of God to our everyday lives?

DON'T GO TO HELL FROM THE CHURCH

Their will always be Preachers in the Pulpit preaching to others and they are on their way to hell. PEOPLE PLEASE DON'T GO TO HELL FROM THE CHURCH. Your soul is more valuable than that.

Let we ask you a question? What is your reason for going to church every Sunday? Is it to meet the deacon in the finance room after church? Is it to meet the preacher so he can take you to your favorite hotel? Is it to look at somebody else husband or wife?

CHURCH FOLKS GONE WILD!

I was talking to a young man and he told me one reason he didn't want to go to church anymore is because there are too many hookers in church. This is sad when somebody label church folks as this.

AGAIN, CHURCH FOLKS GONE WILD. BEWARE OF CHURCH FOLKS!

There is a difference between CHURCH FOLKS and GOD'S FOLKS

Come on, Yes this kind of foolishness is going on right in the house of the lord. You've got preachers with a wife and a girlfriend; they justify by saying look how many wives Solomon had. Look how many concubines he had.

DON'T GO TO HELL FROM THE CHURCH.

STOP BELIEVING THESE LIES FROM THE PULPIT.

Members are sleeping with members, men sleeping with

men, women sleeping with women and we wonder why our children are so messed up. That's just straight nasty, Spiritual incest; sleeping with your sisters and brothers in the house of God, and you wonder why sinners don't want any part of the church. How can you be an effective leader when you sleeping with your church members that comes to you for counseling? It's time to stop sleeping in somebody else bed on Friday and Saturday nights and then go home to your wife on Sunday morning. CHURCH FOLKS GONE WILD!

I've got something for you lady preachers as well. You got a husband and a boyfriend; now tell me what does God say about it? You treat the preacher better than you treat your husband. You will go get water for the pastor, but can't bring water to your own husband; Yes God got a problem with that. God is giving you time to repent. If you don't repent and you die in your sin you are going straight to hell.

PLEASE DON'T GO TO HELL FROM THE CHURCH.

The church is getting more wicked and wicked as time goes by. God's wrath is about to come down on the church like never before. We never know the day or the hour when the son of man shall appear in all His Glory. We need to be ready when He calls our name.

God wants His people to repent and turn from their wicked ways. Sometimes it takes hell on earth to get people to repent. God is coming sooner than we think. God has already told us in His word that warning comes before destruction. We see all the warning signs around us, but yet and still we fail to obey the word of God. WHY

ARE WE STILL PLAYING WITH GOD? GOD AIN'T PLAYING WITH ANY OF US.

Don't be the devils assistant. He's roaming around seeking whom he can devour. We love to say that the devil is busy, but guess who's giving him work to do? THE SAINTS! We are the ones that have the devil working overtime. He is doing his job, but when is the church going to start doing our job?

We are living in a time where people think its ok as long as you are a Christian you can live any kind of way. Who told you that lie? False teachers telling people what they want to hear and not what they need to hear. There are consequences for sin. There are consequences for disobeying God. There are consequences for doing your thang when you want to do it. Keep playing with God and see don't you get burnt. Fire burns whether you know it or not.

We are in a spiritual battle and we cannot fight this battle in the natural. It's time to put on our war clothes and keep them on. You never know when the devil will try to attack you. Look at what the scripture says:

Ephesians 6:10-18King James Version (KJV)

[10] Finally, my brethren, be strong in the Lord, and in the power of his might.

[11] Put on the whole armour of God that ye may be able to stand against the wiles of the devil.

[12] For we wrestle not against flesh and blood, but against

principalities, against powers, against the rulers of the darkness of this world, against spiritual wickedness in high places.

¹³ Wherefore take unto you the whole armour of God that ye may be able to withstand in the evil day, and having done all, to stand.

¹⁴ Stand therefore, having your loins girt about with truth, and having on the breastplate of righteousness;

¹⁵ And your feet shod with the preparation of the gospel of peace;

¹⁶ Above all, taking the shield of faith, wherewith ye shall be able to quench all the fiery darts of the wicked.

¹⁷ And take the helmet of salvation, and the sword of the Spirit, which is the word of God:

¹⁸ Praying always with all prayer and supplication in the Spirit, and watching thereunto with all perseverance and supplication for all saints;

Do you really believe what these passages of scripture are saying? We've always got to keep on our armor. It is not about you; God wants us to put on the whole armor of God so that we will be able to stand in the evil days which we are living.

When we are unarmed, we are very weak and easily beaten down. The devil wants to keep us down.

We must remember that our weapons of our warfare are

not carnal, but mighty through the pulling downs of strongholds.

We are armed with the most powerful weapon there is and that is the word of God. I think sometimes we don't even realize what we're holding or how powerful our weapon really is. We are carrying life and death in our hands. How many of you know we are living in a time where the saints really need to be encouraged in the Lord. The devil is doing all he can to sift us all like wheat, but we have an anchor in Christ Jesus. I know the road gets rough sometimes and the going gets tough sometimes, but we got to learn how to stand. Oppositions are going to come, but we got to stand, we're going to be criticized and lied on, but we've got to stand anyway. Payday is coming after while if we don't quit, if we don't give in, if we don't throw in the towel. Victory belongs to the saints of God. We have no reason to walk around with our heads all hung down feeling sorry for ourselves. We are children of the Most-High God.

As you continue to read this book, I want to encourage you to stay in the race, don't look to the left or the right, but keep your eyes on Jesus. We are living in a time where Satan will do all he can to distract the people of God, but whatever you do keep your eyes on the Lord.

The race is not given to the swift neither to the strong, but it's given to them that endure until the end, so don't give up and don't give in because God has already equipped you for the battle.

Stop fighting your brother. Stop fighting your sister. Stop fighting the preacher. Stop fighting your husband or your wife. Stop fighting your children. Stop fighting your grandchildren, Stop fighting your friends. It really isn't them. The real enemy is Satan and we can't even recognize him when he shows up.

When you have done all you can, do stand anyway. Stand when oppositions arise in your life. Stand when chaos is all around you. You might have to stand through some hard times but stand anyway. God will see you through. The devil wants to cause confusion in your life. The devil wants you to think you will never amount to anything.

DON'T SAY YOU HAVEN'T BEEN WARNED...Whatever you do, DON'T GO TO HELL FROM THE CHURH.

CHAPTER 5

GOD WILL GIVE YOU DIRECTION

Every morning I get a devotional from a dear friend of mine in Irmo, South Carolina. I would like to share this with my readers.

God's Word –which is our Road Map: "Thy word is a lamp unto my feet, and a light unto my path." Psalm 119:105

MEDITATION: When traveling in your car, the latest devices drivers use is the GPS or MapQuest. Sometimes these devices have made mistakes or will take us away from our destination. Along with my lady friends, we were traveling to a destination in Charlotte North Carolina a few months ago, the GPS just could not get us to our destination, and finally we asked another driver to lead us to our destination.

God's word is our map from earth to heaven. His word shows us what paths to follow in our daily conduct and service. When you open your Bible everyday, you don't have to worry about errors, omissions or mistakes, the Bible is our complete guide. Every word is trustworthy; every chapter will lead us safely home. To the believers that is good news! Today, share this good news with someone in your path, and share this good news with your family and friends. This is a prayer for you.

PENELOPE "MINISTER P." TAYLOR

PRAYER

Dear Lord, we thank you for your word.
Thank You that we have your word as our
Guide for daily living. Lord, help us to
Make time to read and study your word
So that we can make it safely home to you.
In Jesus Name Amen

By Vera Starks
Irmo, South Carolina

I wanted to share this because we all need direction in our life. We seek the wrong people for direction, and they can't even help themselves, but Jesus is our road map that leads us to heaven.

There is trouble all around us. Children acting crazy, women want to be men, men want to be women. Look at the world, it is in a mess, but don't you get sidetrack. Don't get distracted because the devil wants to keep your mind occupied with all kind of junk.

A friend of mine has really being going through a rough time with her daughter, but I do believe that God is about to deliver her daughter out of her situation. Our children will go through situations that we feel like they cannot handle, and nobody can help them, but I told my friend that the God we serve is able to deliver her daughter out of anything. That's a good way for the devil to keep us distracted by trying to get next to our children. There will be times we will have to go to God and ask Him to give our children direction because sometimes they are blind to what God is trying to do in their lives. It's time we give our children back to the Lord because He can handle them better than we can. Why are you letting your children run your blood pressure up? Why are you letting your children keep you stressed out for reasons you have no control over? Why would you want to live in hell and then die and go to hell? PLEASE DON'T GO TO HELL FROM THE CHURH.

So many people complain about what they don't have instead of thanking God for what He has already blessed them with. If you really want to be blessed look in the word of God and see what it says about blessings.

Stop being Jealous when God bless somebody else. If you can be happy for them then I know your blessings will come. Sometimes God will not bless us because we are not happy when He blesses somebody else. Some people want to be blessed but don't want to go through anything to get the blessings. You might see a person's Glory, but you don't understand their story. Stop judging a person by what you see on the outside. I have found looks to be very deceiving. Looks are deceiving to God as well that's why He judges the heart. Now is the time to seek direction from God in all aspects of your life. God already knows everything about us before we even ask Him. We serve an awesome God who is able to deliver and set us free.

 A lot of us love social media, I know I do because I have a Facebook ministry, but people please stop telling Facebook every detail of your life. There are stalkers, murders, and child molesters all over Facebook lurking on your Facebook page. If you want to tell someone your entire business, try telling it to somebody that can really help you and His name is JESUS. He will give you Directions.

PENELOPE "MINISTER P." TAYLOR

CHAPTER 6

KEEP IT MOVING

God told Joshua the same thing I gave to Moses I have given to you. Look at what the scripture says...

Joshua chapter 1 verse 1-7 reads

Now after the death of Moses the servant of the LORD it came to pass, that the LORD spake unto Joshua the son of Nun, Moses' minister, saying,

2 Moses my servant is dead; now therefore arise, go over this Jordan, thou, and all this people, unto the land which I do give to them, even to the children of Israel.

God was letting Joshua know, Moses have died, but I still got work for you to do. It's time out for sitting around feeling sorry for yourself, get up and KEEP IT MOVING

3 Every place that the sole of your foot shall tread upon, that have I given unto you, as I said unto Moses.

Everything God gave to Moses to get the Job done he is now giving to Joshua and whatever God has for you to do He will equip you for the task at hand.

4 From the wilderness and this Lebanon even unto the great river, the river Euphrates, all the land of the Hittites,

and unto the great sea toward the going down of the sun, shall be your coast.

God had already told him what coast he needed to take. God had already made the way for Joshua.

[5] There shall not any man be able to stand before thee all the days of thy life: as I was with Moses, so I will be with thee: I will not fail thee, nor forsake thee.

Now when God tell you this, you better keep it moving. He said I will be with you and I will not fail you. When you know that God is with you it makes your assignment that much easier. When you know that God is with you it does not matter what the naysayers have to say. It doesn't matter what the haters have to say. All you need to do is KEEP IT MOVING.

We've got to many people in the body of Christ that likes to keep mess going. It's time to grow up and stop letting every little thing wear you out. One reason a lot of people can't keep it moving is because they are so caught up on the past. What somebody said about me, what somebody did to me last year? Yesterday is gone and tomorrow is not promised, but what you can do is start from where you are now and begin to seek God for the things that are not right in your life. No matter what's going on in your life if you seek God, He will see you through. We need to ask God to order our steps and give us direction. It's not time to PLAY church it's time to PRAY church.

If you want to live a holy righteous life you need to get in the word of God and see what God has to say about being Holy. Everything we need to know about Godly living is in the word of God. One reason our life is so messed up is because we want to do things our way instead of God's way. God's way is always far better than our way. This Christian Journey is not like burger king, you can't have it your way. If you want to live a prosperous life. I dare you to get in the word of God. God does not want His children standing still. We need to move from where we are to better things God has in store for us.

I want to ask my readers a Question. Why are you still letting the devil beat you down? Go to the word of God and look at John 10:10 Listen what it says, talking about the devil, your adversary. He comes to steal, kill, and destroy, but I like the part that Jesus says. Jesus says I come that you might have life and have it more abundantly. It's time out for letting the devil steal your Joy, your happiness, and your peace. It's time to rejoice in the Lord. It's time to get in the word of God and believe what His word has to say about you.

If you really believe what this word is saying you wouldn't be so BROKE, BUSTED, AND DISCUSSED. You wouldn't be so BEAT DOWN, and BROKE DOWN. It's time for the body of Christ to get in your rightful place in God. It's time to come up out of that down trotting spirit. It's time to come up out of that lustful spirit. It's time to come up out of that Homosexual Spirit. It's time to come up out of that Jealous Spirit. It's time to come up out of that Adulterous spirit. I'm calling the row. Have I got to your row yet? It's time out or playing Church. We got to many monkeys in the house of the Lord playing church. Recess is over. Church is not entertainment tonight. Church is not happy hour, Church is not a circus. Church is not club HUSH, that's a club in my city just in case somebody wants to know. God is not playing with us, time is winding down. It's time for the body of Christ to begin too live according to God's standard and not mans! It's time to stop feeling sorry for yourself because nobody else does. It's time to stop letting the devil beat you down. It's time to keep it moving. Get up from where you are and begin to do something right. It's time for the body of Christ to stop sucking on sour lemons and begin to eat some sweet grapes. ENOUGH is ENOUGH! It's time for you to KEEP IT MOVING!

Chapter 7

PUNKS AND PIMPS IN THE PULPIT

Some of you are not going to like this message, but I promise if you're living this lifestyle it aught to make you want to change. I'm not going to give you my opinion or what I think, I'm going to go to the word of God and tell you what thus says the Lord. Please readers, you don't have to go to HELL FROM THE CHURCH. I urge you to share this book with your family, your co-workers and your friends.

There are too many leaders allowing Sissies and Punks in God's Holy Place, and GUESS WHAT? God is going to hold leaders accountable. Don't get me wrong they need to go to church and seek deliverance, but they shouldn't be able to hold a position until there heart is right before God. Leaders you KNOW they are a sissy, but you allow then in the pulpit anyway. You KNOW they are a punk and you allow them to preach over God's people. You KNOW they are shacking up. but you still allow them to be over the singles ministry or the married couples ministry. I'm going to say this again.

Leaders I want you to KNOW God is going to hold you accountable for how you handle His bride which is the church. There are so many people in the body of Christ that think they can do as they please, say what they want, do what they want and still think they are going to heaven. People let's not get it twisted. The word of God says in Hebrews 12:14 Follow peace with all *men*, and holiness, without which no man shall see the Lord:" DON'T GO TO HELL FROM THE CHURCH!

God wants us to live at peace with all men if possible. We've got to be Holy if we want to see Jesus. We can't live like a junk yard dog and think we will make it into heaven. Ministers sitting in the pulpit with them tight skinny jeans on and that little ole coat is not showing Holiness. We come into God's house looking any old way, but we make excuses by saying God says come as you are, but you don't go in the court room as you are, you are going to tuck your shirt in and you are going to be neatly dress, well why can't we do the same for God's house? Skinny jeans have their place but not in the pulpit.

God want us to be Holy and if we say we are a child of the king we need to carry ourselves like we are a child of the king at all times. Do you ever wonder why people are leaving our churches and going back into the world? One reason is because our leaders and church folks are not living a life of Holiness unto God.

We can't preach what we're not living. I constantly tell my Facebook ministry PRACTICE what you PREACH or SHUT UP! People are watching what we say, what we do and how we carry ourselves. The world is looking at us. If we are professing Jesus Christ, we will be under a microscope. We can't say we are a child of God and we have a wife and a girlfriend; we can't say we are a child of God and we want to run the church, but we can't even run our own household. We can't say we are a child of God and we been shacking up with someone else's husband or wife for the last 20-30 years.

Where is the real Church? We can't try to control God's people when we can't control our own children. People whatever you do DON'T GO TO HELL FROM THE CHURCH. This book is tight, but I know its right. God has given me these nuggets to help somebody along the way and let you know that there is life after death and you DON'T HAVE TO GO TO HELL FROM THE CHURCH. You really don't have to go to hell at all. If you end up in hell it will be nobody fault but your own.

God has given us the road map to live a successful Christian life, but it's up to us to use the road map that He has given each one of us. Don't get me wrong God loves Punks and Pimps but stop saying God made you that way. You need to go back to the beginning and see that God made Adam and Eve, He made male and female and He wouldn't have it any other way. You can change, you can come out of that lifestyle, you don't have to continue a lifestyle that God never intended for you to be in, but the devil will do all he can to keep you living that lifestyle which you know yourself is an abomination unto God.

Most of us were raised up in the church and we know the way, but somewhere along the way we got off track, you got sidetrack, but you don't have to stay there. Today is your day to come out. The devil will whisper in your ear that's its ok to stay there, but your spirit man knows the truth, so today let your spirit man override your flesh so you can be set FREE!

John 8:36 says if the Son therefore shall MAKE you free, ye

shall be free indeed."

It is Jesus Christ who makes us FREE, we can do nothing unless the father draws us. Will you let Him draw you today? If you are reading this book it is no accident. This book was Predestine with you in mine.

Repeat this prayer: Father God in the name of Jesus I know I have sinned against you in my body, mind and soul, but father God I am asking right now that you deliver me and set me free. God I'm sorry for the things I have done to my body and in my body, but God I know if I ask you will cleanse me from all unrighteousness you will forgive me and remember my sins no more in Jesus name I pray. Amen

If you prayed this prayer in faith and believed in your heart that God has freed you, so walk in it and give God some Praise. Now get under good leadership where you can grow in Grace, and in the things God would have you to do for the kingdom.

Chapter 8

THUGS IN THE CHURCH

Some of you readers may be wondering where I'm going with this subject. Keep reading, because yes there are THUGS IN THE CHURCH.

I looked up the word Thug in the dictionary. It says that a thug is a cruel or vicious person, a robber, or a murderer. Do you know anybody in your church that fits this description? Pastor Christopher Smithson preached a sermon about Thugs in the church. We got a lot of thuggish church folks if the truth be told. We talk about the thugs in the street but what about the thugs in the church, but yet you say you're on your way to heaven. You will walk way across the room to keep from speaking to your sister or your brother. You will fall out, speak in tongues, shout all over the church and get up and roll your eyes at your sister and think you are alright with God. I'm talking about thugs in the church. How many thuggish robbers do we have in the church stealing God's money, going behind closed doors and filling their pockets with God's money? How many thuggish church folks are murdering people with there tongue? When is the church going to start loving people from where they are? Can we as the church love people when they come in stinking from drinking? Can we love people when they come in tore up from the floor up? Can we love people that don't look like us? God want to get that thuggish spirit out of us. Please folks whatever you do DON'T GO TO HELL FROM THE CHURCH. There are so many leaders preaching God's Holy word and on their way to hell. Let me tell you one thing readers, when we stand before God the only person He's going to ask us about is us. Stop staying home from church because of what you heard. Stop staying home from church because of what the preacher is doing. Stop staying home from church because somebody made you mad. If you don't like the church you're apart of leave. I don't know how many churches are in your city but the last time I checked we have over three hundred churches in the city of Waycross, Georgia. Like I said in previous chapters if you go to hell from the church it's nobody fault but your own. God want to bless us in so many ways, but we've got to position ourselves to prosper. God wants to clean up the church.

The word of God says let the wheat and tare grow together and God will do the separating. It is not our job to run people away from the church. God is the one that will separate. It's time for the real church to take a stand. It's time for the real leaders to come forth and take a stand for God, take a stand for righteousness, and take a stand for Holiness. In the end we will be glad we did.

CHAPTER 9

LOOSE WOMEN IN THE CHURCH

I attend a ladies bible class every Monday morning that is taught by an awesome woman of God, Dr. Johnnie Mae Swinson. We are studying right now how to be God's COVER GIRLS, by having a heart after God. We have about thirty to forty women that attend the class every Monday. We are only there for one hour. This class teaches us how to do the work of the ministry. This class teaches us how to be a Titus 2 woman. This class is design to help women from all walks of life, whether you are struggling in your marriage, having problems with your children, your finances, being single or whatever area, you may be weak in. We all have some weak areas in our life and this class is designed for women of all walks of life. I am learning so much from this awesome teacher. She taught a lesson on loose women in the church, and how many of you readers know there are some loose women in the church?

No training, no respect for God or our leaders, loose tongue, we say anything we want when we want. If we learn how to keep our mouths shut our homes will be better, our lives will be changed if we learn how to control our loose tongue, and the only way we can control our tongue is through the power of God. The word of God says in

James 3:8 but the tongue can no man tame; it is an unruly evil, full of deadly poison. How many of you know our tongue can kill a person?

We all need to watch what we say and season our words with love and grace. I thank God He is teaching me when to talk and when to be quiet. I didn't say I've mastered it I said I'm learning. God does not want us to be loose women. Let me tell you all something about loose women and then you can decide if you are one of them loose women.

Loose women are always running up in the pastor's face. That loose woman can acknowledge the Pastor but can't stand His wife. That loose woman can get something for the Pastor to drink but won't get her own husband anything to drink. That loose woman will sit on the front row with that short dress on just to get the Pastors attention. I'm talking about loose women in the church. I'm just trying to help somebody as they read this book. God is sick and tired of us faking it till we make it.

Let me ask you a question? Are you a loose woman? If you are you don't have to be. Ask God to take that loose Spirit away from you.

Ladies how many of you all know that we as women are a trip, jealousy and envy among Gods' women. That should not be. God want us to connect to people by the Spirit and not by our flesh. Seek to know no man by the flesh but know them by the Spirit. We've got to learn how to love each other regardless of what we think our sister have or who we think they are. I'm learning that looks can be deceiving. It's time for us to stop judging a book by its cover. Please do not judge this book by the cover; God has anointed me to write this book to help somebody for such a time as this, for this season. God want us to get equip so we will be able to step into any situation. We will be able to step into the situation where we are needed the most.

Nobody should be sitting in church doing nothing; find out what your Spiritual Gift is and ask God to help you to walk in it. God has a destiny out of this world planned just for you, and ladies you can't afford to be a loose woman when you get there. Their will always be somebody hating on you. Their will always be somebody jealous of you. There will always be somebody criticizing you, but guess what? That's their problem not yours. Stop following up everything the enemy brings to you. If you resist the devil, I promise he will flee from you.

When God has empowered you to prosper there will be persecution, there will be envy, there will be jealousy, but remain faithful and keep your eyes on God. Baby in this season you got to learn how to take a licking and keep on ticking because God got your back. God has given us all an assignment, so don't let anything stop you from doing your God given assignment. There will be days when you feel like quitting and giving up, but stay the course, because God will give you strength for the Journey.

This class will help empower you for the Journey. Whatever you do don't be a loose woman but be a woman of determination.

Prayer: Father in the name of Jesus I come to you right now lifting my sister up before you, Lord whatever she may be going through with as she read this book strengthen her right now, let her know that she is not along and you love her very much. Lord the sister that reads this book let her feel a burden lifted off her as she flips through the pages. Lord Bless her to be a woman of excellence, a woman of dignity, a woman of love in Jesus name I Pray. Amen

Quotes from Dr. Swinson

We want to detox our body, but we need to detox our Spirit.

Life is not to be successful without God

If memory would die you wouldn't have to cry

Don't get so busy with other stuff that you forget your mission and your assignment

It's time to stop being a victim; we've all been mistreated so get over it

We need to be movers and shakers wherever we go

Get Spiritual education according to the bible and not according to man

Women we study everything else, we need to study to be quiet

I hope this chapter and all chapters has been a blessing to you. If you are ever in the Waycross GA area, please stop by and visit Dr. Swinson and her class at the Old Crawford Street School we would love to have you join us.

CHAPTER 10

Nuggets from the Prophet

When the Prophet Speaks

Prophet Clifford Mosley

I have been given permission by the Prophet to share his Nuggets with God's people. When the Prophet speaks a shift takes place. When God speaks things happen. We never know when God has just the right word that we need to hear.

You just can't receive parts of the bible that feels good, you have to eat the whole loaf even the parts that provoke you to come out and be separated.

Listen people, the Anointing make the difference, listen when the hand of God is on your life the witches and warlocks can't stop you.

On December 23rd, 2018 the Prophet gave a word that the year 2019 is going to be a year of new and fresh connections, no longer shall you connect with old wineskin mindsets. It's time to LET GO AND LET GOD!

Woe unto you that turn a blind eye and know to do right but find pleasure in remaining to do wrong. Please DON'T GO TO HELL FROM THE CHURCH!

Leaders when you keep your hands clean you will be at liberty to speak what the Lord tell you and you won't have to worry if they are going to tell what you all just finish doing. Your sin will find you!

WARNING to some of you leaders, God sent you the help but you rejected them because of who they were, nothing will go right until you make contact with them and allow them to RELEASE!

BE STILL AND KNOW THAT I AM GOD and know that I sit high and I'm looking down low. My hand is in the mist of it all. I allowed you to see the betrayal because it was part of your growth says the Spirit of the Lord. Now SHAKE it off and KEEP IT MOVING. The process is working for your good! Allow me to encourage you to trust God even when it hurts!

There is a cry in the land for repentance, believe it or not but people are leaving this world, so I say to you that are reading this book get your house in order. The day you hear God's voice harden not your heart says the Spirit of the Lord? You can be happy for a moment or you can change your mindset and be happy for a lifetime. Speak the life you want to live.

Get your affairs in order in the earth realm, I'm coming back like a thief in the night says the Spirit of the Lord and I will be plucking up one by one and I'm coming with my rewards in my hand, readers will you be ready when Jesus return?

 DON'T GO TO HELL FROM THE CHURCH.

CHAPTER 11

NO MORE EXCUSES

Let me tell you something readers, God is sick and tired of our excuses. Some of you might be wondering what an Excuse is. Well I'm glad you asked.

AN EXCUSE IS A REASON YOU GIVE IN ORDER TO EXPLAIN WHY SOMETHING HAS BEEN DONE OR HAS NOT BEEN DONE, OR IN ORDER TO AVOID DOING SOMETHING.

The list of excuses is endless, but God does not want us to keep making excuses for why we can't do anything.

It's easy for us to come up with excuses, that way we want have to blame ourselves for not doing something. It's easy to blame momma nem, it's easy to blame daddy nem. It's easy to blame our siblings. Stop blaming other people for what you didn't do, or what you didn't want to do. If you stop making excuses and just do it you'll wonder what took so long. God has an answer for all of our excuses.

 He has given us Philippians 4:13. My husband and I taught our girls this scripture when they were 4 years old. They are 21, and 23 years old now, but whenever they would say what they CAN'T DO, I would tell them, what does Philippians 4:13 says?

I can do all things through Christ which strengthens me. So, if we really believe this scripture why are we sweating the small stuff? Why do we keep making the same old excuses over and over again?

Look at people in the bible that made excuses, starting with Adam and Eve back in the book of genesis, playing the blame game. They had to blame somebody accept themselves. They said the same thang flip Wilson said... THE DEVIL MADE ME DO IT. How many times do we say the devil made me do it?

NO! One reason we didn't do it is because we was too lazy, or we was too tired, or we was too sleepy, or whatever other excuse we want to come up with.

In the Christian world we can find all kind of excuses not to obey God. How many of you feel guilty as you read this?

Ben Franklin wrote, He that is good for making excuses is seldom good for anything else.

Look what Moses said to the Lord. I am a nobody and I am not qualified to go to Pharaoh and demand the release of God's people. How many of us feel this way? Feels like you are not as qualified as someone else or that you just don't have the ability to get the job done properly. Sometimes we give up before we ever get started. We all are trained real good at making excuses. I don't know how. I don't understand. I have a doctor's appointment. My children have homework. EXCUSES, EXCUSES, EXCUSES.

God is sick and tired of our excuses people.

DO YOU KNOW THAT EVERYTIME YOU MAKE AN EXCUSE IT SLOWS YOU DOWN?

Look at the man sitting by the pool of Bethesda for 38 long years, making excuses for why he couldn't get in the water. Some of us have been making the same excuse far to long.

Don't get stuck in life looking to blame somebody else for the mistakes you caused.

Your momma told you that joker wasn't any good before you married him, but because you kept making excuses for why you needed him in your life you found out the hard way. You just had to have him. Now you are catching the devil with him. Now you found out momma was telling the truth.

So why are you still blaming momma? Why are you still blaming Daddy? None of us can do anything about our past, but we can do something about our NOW!

STOP BLAMING THE PEOPLE THAT HURT YOU, YOU'VE HURT SOME PEOPLE TOO.

Stop crying over spilled milk and get a towel and wipe it up. I declare and decree that the things that have held you back are coming to an end in Jesus name.

Let's all make a vow this day. NO MORE EXCUSES.

PENELOPE "MINISTER P." TAYLOR

CHAPTER 12

PUT A PRAISE ON IT

As we entered into year 2019, I knew there are some things I just needed to put a PRAISE ON! I will be doing a women's conference this year entitle "PUT A PRAISE ON IT" Some things God just want to put a seal on and let you know that it's already done in Jesus name.

No matter what we are going through we still got a right to give God some Praise. God has been better to us than we ever thought about being to ourselves. It's time for us as the body of Christ to stop being so selfish, always thinking about ourselves, what about me. I hear God saying YES WHAT ABOUT YOU? God knows everything about you. It's time for us to stay focus on what really matters in life and that is Jesus Christ. The word of God has already told us that No weapon that is formed against us shall prosper. Stop worrying about petty stuff that has no real meaning.

When you fall you don't stay down, pick yourself up and give God some Praise. If the devil can get you to keep your mouth shut about the things the Lord is doing in your life he will. Stop focusing on the naysayers, stop focusing on the ones that's player hating on you, stop focusing on what other folks are doing and focus on what God has told you to do. It's time out for sowing discord among our sisters and brothers; it's time out for allowing bitterness and jealousy to control your life. It's time out for being envious of one another. Yes, we are our brother's keeper, yes we are our sister's keepers. It's time to be all that God has called us to be. I know some of you that are reading this book have had some hard times, we all have, but instead of complaining find a way to give God some PRAISE!!

Stop looking at what the next person is doing; get your eyes set on God so you can do something good. I know some of you might be saying, Well Minister P. you don't know my situation. Well Minister P. you don't know how bad they hurt me, and you are so right I don't know but I know a man that does know and His name is Jesus; all you got to do is turn your situation over to him and I declare he will fix it for you.

SOMETIMES WE GOT TO BE LIKE DAVID AND LEARN HOW TO ENCOURAGE OURSELVES. STOP WAITING ON OTHER PEOPLE TO VALIDATE YOU. STOP WAITING ON OTHER PEOPLE TO PAT YOU ON THE BACK. STOP WAITING ON OTHER PEOPLE TO SAY SOMETHING NICE ABOUT YOU. WHY? BECAUSE THEY JUST MIGHT NOT.

Get in God's word and see what He has to say about you. He says you are fearfully and wonderfully made. He says you are a lender and not a borrower. He says you are more than a conqueror through Christ Jesus. He says you are the head and not the tail. What else do I need to tell you before you believe what God has to say about you? Go to the B.I.B.L.E. Basic Instructions, Before Leaving Earth. God has given us His road map on how to live a happy successful life in Christ.

I have a Facebook ministry and I do a morning word to encourage the people of God as they head off to work and for those that are home bound. Let me share a Monday through Friday encouragement just for you. Take this book with you so that no matter what day you are feeling down you can pick this book up and look at the word for that day.

Monday is MOTIVATED MONDAY

As you read this devotional you got to learn how to keep yourself motivated to keep it moving. I don't care what your body is telling you today stay motivated. I don't care what your mind is telling you to do stay motivated. I don't care what the naysayers are saying about you today stay motivated.

I know you feel like giving up, but today is not the day, and tomorrow is not promised. Stay in the race. Keep your head up and keep moving forward, you are almost at the finish line, but if you give up today you will never make it to the finish line. Some of us have gotten so complacent, but we got to stay motivated and keep it moving.

Some of us are stuck in churches being in our comfort zone when we know God has told us to get up and move, but because my momma name is on a window and my daddy name is on a pew I'm not going anywhere. Let me tell you something readers, as long as you stay in that dark place God can't use you. Jesus is light and He is the light of the world. Please don't give up on God because God will never give up on you. Whatever you do stay Motivated.

What is the Lord speaking to your Spirit?

_____
_____

_____

Tuesday is TERRIFIC TUESDAY

You can have a terrific day, but the choice is up to you. Don't get discouraged when the enemy comes in like a flood, because we have good news the spirit of the lord will raise up a standard against the enemy. God has more to offer us than the devil ever will. You don't have to get out of bed acting like somebody peed in your cornflakes. God is more than enough. Don't let the devil win in your lIfe. You are too valuable to God. Remember that many of the afflictions are of the righteous but the lord will deliver us from them all. WE CAN SHOUT RIGHT THERE! If God be for you who can be against you? God is faithful to his word. With that being said you can have a terrific Tuesday.

What is the Lord speaking to your Spirit?

_____

_____

_____

Wednesday is WINNING WEDNESDAY

We are victorious through Christ Jesus. You are a winner through Christ Jesus. The only way you are a loser is if you want to be. Some of us have been told all our life we will never be anything, by parents or even by someone you looked up to. Stop believing the lies of the enemy.

Stop letting the enemy tell you, you are not a winning. When you really, really know who you are in Christ and believe what the word of God says about you the enemy can't touch you. The devil would love for you to give up in the middle of your race, but you've come too far to give up now. How many of you want to win today?

You've got to do something to win. We say we are victorious, but do we really believe what we are saying? Are you winning today? You can't win lying on the sofa all day long watching the soap opera, you can't win playing video games or candy crush all day long, and you can't win partying and drinking all day long, stop being mad and angry because someone else is winning.

Get up off your lazy behind; go get a job and stop being complacent. If God did it for them He's the same God that can and will do it for you. Let me encourage you by saying hold on just a little while longer, don't get weary in doing what's right because in due season God will give you the benefits you deserve. I declare and decree that this is your winning season.

What is the Lord speaking to your Spirit?

Thursday is THANKFUL THURSDAY

How many thankful readers do I have today? Are you thankful that when God made this day He made it with you in mind? He could have cut us off last night but He spared us another chance to get right with him and with our sisters and our brothers. Are you Thankful? Their is nobody on the face of this earth that has done what God has done for each one of us. Who woke you up this morning? Who put food on your table? Who gave you a job? Who keeps you from drowning? Yes God is my lifeguard, so when I feel like I am drowning I always know that I have someone that will always come to my rescue. We got to learn how to thank God for things being as well as it is because things can always be worse. Yes I am very thankful, so the next time you feel like complaining remember where your help comes from.

What is the Lord speaking to your Spirit?

Friday is FABULOUS FRIDAY

Well, well, well we're now at the fifth day for our devotional. My prayer is that you are getting delivered as you read and meditate on these nuggets that I have designed through the word of God to help you have a fabulous day. Some of us need God to turn some things around in our life. You thought you could handle it on your own, but then you discovered the problem was too big for you to handle. God is our very present help in our times of trouble. You are going to have trials, you are going to have tribulations, but let God be your first source and not your last source. God is the one that causes us to have a fabulous day. The more of God's word we get on the inside of us the better our day will be. If God has allowed us to see another day we should to make it a fabulous day.

What is the lord speaking to your Spirit?

_____
_____
_____
_____
_____
_____

I pray that this book will encourage you to know that you don't have to go to hell from the church. God laid this title on my heart for such a time as this. Some preachers will not preach what is written in this book. God has anointed me to preach the word in season, and out of season. He has anointed me to preach when the people want to hear the truth and to preach when they don't want to hear the truth. Thanks to every reader that invested and will invest in this book. My prayer is that God will richly bless your life as he has promised in Matthew 6:33 to them that obey him.

I am so blessed by God to be able to complete my third book. My Husband and I will be retiring from our fulltime job on May 31, 2019. My Prayer is that God will bless the next chapter of our life in ways we never dreamed of. Readers whatever you dream of doing do it now because tomorrow is not promised to any of us. God really does want to bless us, but we have to do something to receive God's blessings. If you don't go to work you want receive a paycheck, it's just that simple. Do something for God and God will do something for you. If you don't put anything in the bank you want get anything out. Learn how to serve God, and trust me God will serve you. God will take you places you never dreamed of going. God will show you things you never thought about seeing. God will give you the desires of your heart when you walk upright before Him. God said I had to have three books completed before I retire, so God here it is.

Thank you all for taking the time to read this book because it is blessed of the Lord.

Much Love

Minister P.

ABOUT THE AUTHOR

Minister P. as she is affectionally called was born and raised in the city of Waycross, Georgia where she resides there. She is a 1978 graduate of Waycross High School in Waycross, Georgia. She is married to the love of her life of 38 years, together they have 3 children, 2 grandchildren and one Great Grandson.

She is a dedicated member of Walking by Faith Ministry under the Leadership of Pastor Billy and Minister LaWanda Taylor. She was licensed to Preach the Gospel on July 27, 2013, she does not mind preaching what thus says the Lord

She is the founder and C.E.O. of Women of Destiny, a Ministry God birthed out of her on April 20, 2013. Her mission is to help bring healing to women from all walks of life who are hurting and feel that all hope is gone.

She's a Published author of "TRUST GOD NO MATTER WHAT" "HOW PENNIE GOT HER GROOVE BACK" and "DON'T GO TO HELL FROM THE CHURCH."

She also has a $5.00 PAPARAZZI JEWERLY business under the name of MINISTER PS BOUTIQUE. You can visit her website at www.ministerpsboutique.com. God is doing something Awesome in this season

PENELOPE "MINISTER P." TAYLOR

CONTACT INFORMATION

Email address:

<u>pennietaylor10@gmail.com</u>

Facebook Name

Pennie Taylor

Mailing Address is:

Penelope "MINISTER P. "Taylor

P.O. BX 2344

Waycross, GA 31502

www.ingramcontent.com/pod-product-compliance
Lightning Source LLC
Chambersburg PA
CBHW070655050426
42451CB00008B/371